Help For Hurting Parents:

Dealing with the Pain of Teen Pregnancy

PO Box 6925
Louisville, KY 40206

August 5, 1997

Dear Reader,

As this second printing of *Help for Hurting Parents* goes to press, we look back on our own experience with both joy and concern. Our daughter, the one whose situation begin our work in this ministry, was married just two months ago. She has graduated from college where she was on the dean's list and is now beginning a new and exciting chapter in her life.

Five years ago, though, she was devastated. Having just begun college, she was home ten days later to break the news to us that she was going to have a baby. The memory of that evening is still fresh in my mind, and it seems as though it were yesterday. Yet the pain of that time has subsided and yielded to the joy which we have experienced as a result of our family's growth through the ordeal. Because our own memory is still so fresh, we would like to say to you that we know your pain. At the risk of sounding a bit "preachy," I want to offer you a word of hope: God loves you and has not abandoned you. You may think he has left you, I know I thought the same thing at times. In retrospect though we have been able to recognize the fact that God's hand was at work all along, guiding us even when we did not realize it. The Bible tells us that God says, "Never will I leave you; never will I forsake you" (Hebrews 13:5). To that we add our own word of personal testimony affirming that truth.

It is our prayer that this booklet may be helpful to you in sorting out your feelings and emotions. We know how important it is during times like these to have someone who really does know your journey. We invite you to write us if you wish. From time to time we have received letters and calls from parents, and we do respond to those. So please do write if you wish. Meantime, may God bless you during this time.

Sincerely,

Help For Hurting Parents:
Dealing with the Pain of Teen Pregnancy

Scripture taken from the HOLY BIBLE, NEW INTERNATIONAL VERSION. Copy-
right ©1973, 1978, 1984 International Bible Society. Used by permission of Zondervan
Bible Publishers.

Chapter 1

Initial Shock

But we have this treasure in jars of clay to show that this all-surpassing power is from God and not from us. 2 Cor. 4:7

In 1992 my family and I moved to Louisville, Kentucky so that I could follow God's call into Christian ministry by first preparing through seminary studies. We had barely unpacked the U-Haul truck when we had to deal with a crisis – teen pregnancy. This wasn't supposed to be happening. We had followed God's leadership, changed careers, and relocated. Now this. We were broken.

In his second letter to the Christians at Corinth the Apostle Paul compares the human being to a frail, breakable, clay pot. Few events in the life of the Christian family portray that clay-pot nature more than when a teenage, unwed daughter says, "I'm pregnant!" To complicate matters, this is not one of the things we plan and prepare for in life. We know that death and sickness will touch our family, so we prepare in advance as much as possible. We know that our children will grow up and leave home one day, so we prepare for that. What we don't prepare for though is for our precious daughters to become pregnant out of turn. That's not supposed to happen, and when it does we discover just how much our jars really are made of clay. Before despairing over that fact, note how Paul continues: "...to show that this all-surpassing power is from God ...." God has not insulated us from the effects of the world in which we live, nor has he rendered us incapable of sinning and experiencing the effects of sin, but he has promised us the power to deal with our circumstances.

1

Since you are reading this book you probably have already experienced (or know someone who has experienced) the shock of hearing the words "I'm pregnant" from an unwed teenager. This is the kind of experience that jolts a parent and immediately threatens all the hopes and dreams parents have for their daughter. It is as though you suddenly discover that your lives are made of clay pots that have just been shattered. All plans seem now to be suspended, priorities are changed, and the future is just a question mark.

The problems of being a parent come with the territory. Raising a child is usually a joyous labor. From the beginning, parents plan for and expect the best of everything for their children. The last thing most parents would ever expect is that their daughter would become pregnant out of wedlock. Yet the reality is that over one million teenage girls do become pregnant in the United States every year, and half of those pregnancies will end in abortions. The pressures young people experience today are powerful and come from many avenues. The motto of the advertising industry seems to be "Sex sells," and that motto is applied in television, print advertising, outdoor advertising, product packaging, and just about every other form of written communication. Then there are the effects of those in society who advocate distribution of condoms and birth control pills like they were bubble gum. The message from those groups seems to be, "Try sex." Peer pressure also has a profound influence on teenagers, and according to some published reports, more that half of all teenagers engage in premarital sex – and sex often results in pregnancy. As much as teenage pregnancy is a shock to parents, it can be more of a shock to the daughter. She probably had no intention of becoming pregnant, and she has even less idea what to do about it. Most likely she will be scared, confused, and have little knowledge of what needs to be done to take care of herself and the baby. Her life has just taken a turn that stands everything on end. So, no one planned for it. The good news is that it can be dealt with in a positive way; it does not need to be the end of the world. You as a parent need to know that, and your daughter needs to know that.

Putting It In Perspective

Everyone makes mistakes. Usually we are lucky in that only a few people know about our mistakes. Often the guilty party may be the only one who knows because we can hide the evidence. Pregnancy is different. A pregnant teenager cannot hide her condition. It's out there for everybody to see and talk about, and it gets more obvious as time goes by. Nothing short of abortion (or miscarriage) hides the fact that your daughter is pregnant. As a parent you know very well that your daughter's condition will be out there for people to see. That, of course, is a large part of the problem – people *will* see and notice that your daughter is pregnant.

After our daughter told us that she was pregnant, the thing I thought most about was not **her** mistake, but my own long history of mistakes and failures. Every time I was tempted to criticize her I could think instead only of my own list of sins. The longer I concentrated on her failure, the more God reminded me of my own transgressions. I also thought about the fact that my sins were largely unknown to those around me. I could go to work, school, or church smiling, and no one would know all the sins that I had committed. Not so for Louise; the evidence of her mistake, her sin, would be out front (literally) for everyone to see. It would be there at school, at church, shopping, and everywhere else. There would never be a time in the months that followed that the evidence was not there and visible. In order even to begin to experience what she would go through I would need to make a big sign advertising at least one of my worst sins, hang it around my neck, and wear it for nine months. As a parent having discovered that your teenage daughter is pregnant, try this exercise: sit down and make a list of your own worst sins, the things you would be most humiliated to have even one other person know about. Then imagine wearing a sign around your neck announcing one of those sins to *everyone you know*. You should quickly understand that the important thing is not assigning blame or condemnation, but rather achieving restoration and healing.

It is also important to recognize that having a pregnant teenager is not the end of the world. In the middle of the nightmare it helps to take stock of the positive. Instead of concentrating on what went wrong, try listing on a sheet of paper what went right. If your daughter came to you for help you should count that as an enormous blessing. For starters, it's an acknowledgment on her part that she needs you. In our own case we had much to be thankful for in spite of the shock:

- our daughter was healthy

- she had not had an abortion

- she came home for help.

So many things had gone right in the face of that one wrong event that we had to thank God even in the midst of our pain. As we thought during the days that followed of all the possible things she might have done, we were just relieved and grateful that she had come home. Take some time as parents to assess what went right *after* your daughter discovered her pregnancy. Then as parents give thanks to God for those things.

Resolve To Be An Asset

As a parent of a pregnant teen, you have the opportunity to demonstrate mercy the same way Jesus did. In the story of the woman caught in the act of adultery, the men who caught her took her to Jesus to see what action he would order. The Law, they reminded Him, required that she be stoned. The woman didn't deny her guilt, and Jesus didn't excuse it. He simply challenged them that whichever one of them was without sin should be the first to begin casting stones. Realizing that none of them qualified, they all went away. Then Jesus said to her, "Neither do I condemn you.... Go now and leave your life of sin" (John 8:11). Your daughter probably knows that she has made a mistake, so she doesn't need to be tormented about it. What she does need is your help. You can choose to be an asset to your daughter or a handicap. Right now she needs you as an asset more than ever. Your initial reaction may be that you don't know how to help her. Don't despair. After all, you were not supposed to have to deal with this; but you are far better equipped to sort through the maze than is your daughter. In the Sermon on the Mount Jesus reminds us that we need not be overcome with fear (Matt. 6:25-34). Even when we don't know the way out of the present circumstance, God knows. When we put our faith in him, even for the challenges we face, we can know that he will guide us through the situation. So, resolve, by faith, to be a helper to your daughter. Don't blame or criticize her; she has probably already done more of that than you can imagine. Instead, reassure her of your unconditional love and concern for her. Then make a pact to go through the pregnancy together, as a family. Let her know that she will never be alone. Resolve as a family to share the burden with one another and to pray together about it. Then trust God for the outcome. Trusting God is your part; working out the result is God's part.

Understanding Her Fears

While you will undoubtedly have many concerns that come to mind very early, remember that your daughter is likely to be consumed with fear. When our daughter informed us that she was pregnant she had just begun college; she had only been there a week and a half. All her plans seemed lost. She was away from home, afraid, and didn't have a clue what to do. Fortunately she had Christian friends who gave her some good advice. They prayed with and for her, and they encouraged her to come home to tell us. After she broke the news to us (and much to her credit) Louise decided to return to college and finish the semester. One of the first things we tried to do was surround her with a support network so that she would know that help was immediately available any time she needed it. One of my instructors at seminary also taught classes at her college, which was one hour away. Even though I had barely met him, I felt he could be a contact point since he drove to her college three times every week. I invited him to coffee one morning to tell him about her situation and ask for help. As we sat in the cafeteria, and with my lips trembling, I explained the situation and asked if he would be willing to be a contact point between Louise and home. One of the things I said to him was that Louise was afraid. His response spoke volumes about his own understanding and compassion. He asked, "Wouldn't you be afraid, too?" Greg's willingness to make contact with Louise and let her know that she had a way home three days a week if needed gave her great peace of mind.

Fear can be crippling. Perhaps the most frightening thing your daughter may anticipate is the fear of losing your love for and confidence in her. You will need to affirm your love for her early and often. The love that the Bible describes is not a conditional love. Instead, the Bible says that God loves us so much that Christ died an ugly death for us. Paul wrote, "But God demonstrates his own love for us in this: While we were still sinners, Christ died for us" (Romans 5:8). So your love for your daughter ought to be a love consisting of action, and a love that is not diminished by her situation. It may sound odd, but you also need to affirm your confidence in her. Remember that your confidence in her probably never was based on any singular action anyway. Instead confidence in a person is based on a pattern of behavior. Don't allow one mistake to overshadow what might otherwise be a significant and positive pattern of behavior.

You and your daughter have probably talked for years about plans for her future. With her pregnancy, those plans now seem totally threatened. She will likely have a fear that the things she and you had hoped for in her future will not come to pass. As a mature adult you have probably had your share of setbacks – in business, college, or elsewhere. Share those with her, and let her know that a temporary delay is not the same as a loss. At a young age something as traumatic as an unexpected pregnancy can seem devastating. Viewed from the perspective of an entire lifetime, nine months is not such a big deal. In fact, your daughter's young age is an advantage in one respect: she has a whole lifetime <u>ahead</u> of her.

Another fear that she will face is, "What will people think and say?" There is no way to answer this in exact terms. With Louise we tried to be honest and straightforward. One night she shared with me her concern that we, as parents, as well as other people, would condemn her for being pregnant and unmarried. First, I assured her that we did not in any way condemn her. Then I acknowledged that there were some people who would look down on her, but that there would be many more who would extend love and compassion. Besides, she was ultimately accountable to God, not to other people. If you will affirm your love and support for your daughter in a non-judgmental way, you will have gone a long way in putting her mind at peace over what other people will think or say.

Perhaps the least pleasant thing to think about is sexually transmitted disease (STD). Without adding to her and your own fears, you should encourage your daughter to be tested for the full range of STDs including the HIV virus. There are two positive reasons for this. First, if the results are negative, to set your minds at ease. Second, if something is detected, to take whatever curative measures can be taken. Many STDs are curable. Further, failure to take early action can in many cases injure the unborn baby.

Another fear your daughter will have is deciding about whether to raise the child or choosing adoption. In the early months of Louise's pregnancy she said on several occasions, "I just feel that the baby is a part of me." All we as parents could say was, "Yes!" There is no point in denying that the baby is a part of the mother. Help your daughter acknowledge her own feelings of attachment and understand that those are normal maternal feelings. In the process, you should let her know that nobody is going to take her baby away from her. Your daughter needs to be allowed and led to make her own decision about the baby's future.

This is a tough one for parents – tough to resist the temptation to tell her what is best for her and the baby. Allow your daughter to make her decision in an environment full of support and absent of pressure. Only then will she feel comfortable asking for your advice and input. This will be discussed more in the next chapter, but for now give your daughter a pressure-free, non-threatening environment.

Dealing With Disappointment

One of my favorite characters in the New Testament is Peter, and one of my favorite passages is Luke 22:31-34 where Jesus predicted that Peter would deny that he even knew Jesus. This occurs of course at the end of Jesus' ministry on earth, after Peter had spent years with Him. Peter had observed Jesus' miracles. Of all the disciples, only Peter had walked on water. He was also with Jesus on the mountain when Jesus was trans-figured. Now Peter was being told that he would commit the cowardly act of denying that he knew Jesus. How Jesus must have been disap-pointed with Peter! Yet Jesus said, "...I have prayed for you, Simon, that your faith may not fail. And when you have turned back, strengthen your brothers" (Luke 22:32). We should each take a close look at Jesus' response to Peter's failure. With the certain knowledge that Peter was about to betray Him, Jesus nevertheless was an encourager. He didn't allow disappointment with Peter or Peter's own failure to interfere with the work that the Holy Spirit would ultimately do through Peter. It would have been easy for Jesus to become very discouraged with Peter. Jesus was facing imminent arrest, trial, and execution. In His prayer the night of His arrest, the Bible tells us that Jesus was in such anguish that "...his sweat was like drops of blood falling to the ground" (Luke 22:44). Jesus certainly had great reason to be disappointed with Peter, yet He didn't allow Peter's failure to affect His own responsibility as a Shepherd. In a like manner, parents have responsibilities toward children that are not cancelled because of a child's behavior.

Disappointment with our children seems to be a natural part of parent-ing. Yet we can be encouraged by the knowledge that God has the power to turn our disappointments into victories. Peter went on to become one of the most powerful instruments of God in the New Testament record, yet when Jesus was being arrested Peter denied that he knew Jesus. Peter's profound failure was not an obstacle to the ultimate work God had in mind for him. How we view disappointment with our children depends on our perspective. With your pregnant daughter, you can react out of hurt pride and count the ways her actions have injured and embarrassed you. Or, you can pray for her, asking God to use the pregnancy in his own way to bring about good. God's power to turn a bad situation into good is still with us today, and it takes us to a new level of faith to trust him with this particular problem. Romans 8:28 still works: "And we know that in all things God works for the good of those who love him, who have been called according to his purpose."

One thing you should do is be honest enough with your daughter to admit that you don't know just how God will work things out. In order for her to grow in faith she needs to know that you are willing to trust God for those things that you don't have answers to yet. You can though, right away, make a decision to trust the entire situation to God. Trusting him means you don't require all the answers; it means you don't need to know what the ultimate resolution will be. Trusting God means allowing him to guide your path and being willing to accept whatever direction he leads you toward. It means trusting his judgment as superior to your own. Finally, when you really trust God, you discover that you can lay your burdens at his feet and walk away from them. What a relief to be relieved of the worry of burdens!

The purpose of this booklet is to give you, the parents, a source of encouragement in order that you may be a helper and friend to your daughter during a time when she desperately needs you. When our daughter became pregnant my wife and I stumbled through the process. During those nine months we discovered that God's hand was actively working in our lives. In the end we had a blessing-filled resolution to a crisis pregnancy. Instead of destroying our family it brought us closer together. Parents of pregnant teenage girls don't have a choice about the fact of the pregnancy, but they do have a choice about how they respond to it. Let me encourage you to respond now by placing your faith for the outcome in God's hands.

Chapter 2

Establish Priorities

Jesus asked him, "What do you want me to do for you?" Luke 18:40–41

In the above passage a blind man had come to Jesus for healing. Seeing him, Jesus asked what he wanted. In our own life situations we often must answer the question, "What do we want?" Until we clearly define our goal we will be unable to make any real progress toward that goal. In a crisis we often get caught up putting out fires all around us without taking time to think through the broader question of where we want our situation to go. When I was in the Marine Corps a fellow officer had a poster on the wall behind his desk. It depicted a man in a swamp trying desperately to climb a tree while an alligator was nipping at his ankles. The caption said something like, "When you're up to your knees in alligators, it's hard to remember that your mission was to drain the swamp." In the early weeks of your daughter's pregnancy you will discover that the alligators are real and they are nipping at your ankles. Don't become discouraged though; there are ways of dealing with alligators. The first thing you need to do is define the primary objective – the goal that you want to work toward in this crisis. You may choose to define that result with different words, but let me share with you the number one priority we established. The primary outcome we wanted to bring about was to have a healthy daughter and a restored family. Notice that our definition doesn't say anything about what to do about the baby. It's not that the baby is unimportant, but that decision is a part of arriving at a healthy daughter and restored family. There would be ample time to make that decision later, but the first item on the agenda was to know where we wanted this all to end emotionally and spiritually.

Healthy Daughter

Your daughter's health involves three dimensions. First is the physical. Pregnancy adds stress to her body and brings about many hormonal changes. This is a time when it is especially important for her to receive proper nutritional and medical care. She needs to be under the care of an obstetrician as soon as possible. You may discover that not all physicians will take on an unwed teenager as a patient. Part of the reason is that teenagers may be considered "high risk" patients requiring special care. The important thing is to find a compassionate and caring physician who will provide ongoing medical care during the term of the pregnancy. It may require asking around to find such a doctor. Don't be afraid to enlist other persons to help. In our case a minister at a church we had visited knew of our situation, and he took the initiative to locate several doctors who came with recommendations. He had already checked with the doctors in advance and found that they would take Louise as a patient.

Concerning the physical changes that your daughter will experience, an excellent resource is the book entitled, *What to Expect When You're Expecting* (see Appendix B). This will help her to understand the body changes that come with pregnancy, because if she doesn't anticipate them they can be frightening to her. When our daughter began to have "morning sickness" she was very alarmed. It will be reassuring to your daughter to know that some of the feelings (physical and emotional) she experiences are normal and won't last forever.

It is very important during the term of the pregnancy that your daughter eat balanced meals. Her doctor may recommend vitamins or other dietary supplements that will help both her and the baby during the pregnancy. Exercise should also be a part of her routine. She should check with her doctor about types of exercise and how much would be appropriate. Also, it is extremely important during the pregnancy that the mother-to-be avoid alcohol, tobacco, and any drugs not prescribed by her doctor. Recent studies suggest that even small amounts of alcohol and tobacco can have adverse effects on the development of the baby. The same is true of drugs, even over-the-counter medications. To be safe, always check with the doctor.

The second dimension of her health is your daughter's emotional state. While you yourself probably feel overwhelmed, your daughter is likely to be even more bewildered. One of her greatest concerns will be that she has lost your love and confidence. You should affirm your love for her early and often, both verbally and by your actions. John 3:16 tells us that God loved us by what he did. We sometimes confuse love and affection. Affection is what we feel, but love is what we do. Jesus taught that we are to love even our enemies. It may be difficult to feel good toward someone who wrongs you, but it is always possible to do for that person what is in his or her best interest. Loving your daughter means caring for her and providing for her needs. She needs to know beyond all doubt that your love for her is not diminished by her pregnancy. She also needs to talk about her feelings and to have parents who are willing to listen. Listening is not always easy, but it can be the most valuable thing we do for someone in pain. You should avoid being eager to give advice early. There will be time for that later, but first you must re-establish and strengthen your relationship with your daughter.

The spiritual dimension is the final component of her health, and it has to do with her relationship with God. We once were contacted by a firm that provided help in securing financial aid for college students. I still remember that the primary device they used for getting our attention was "all the financial aid that is available but goes unclaimed each year." The implication was clear: the *benefits* of that unclaimed financial aid went unclaimed as well. The same is true of forgiveness. God has made the provision for forgiveness for all persons, but for many that forgiveness has gone unclaimed. What a tragedy that freedom from guilt should be so readily available, yet go unclaimed. To suffer from the burden of guilt is debilitating, and guilt is universal. Even animals seem to exhibit guilt. We once had a dog named Beau. Whenever Beau did something wrong he would avoid us. He somehow knew that his actions would be met with disapproval, but then if we smiled and greeted him in a friendly manner (forgiveness) Beau would respond with spontaneous joy. When we suffer from the guilt of sin we impair our relationship with God, and we may try to avoid God because we know we've done wrong. Receiving the forgiveness that God offers can restore our relationship with him and our sense of joy. Jesus died on a cross to pay the penalty of sin; His sacrifice made forgiveness *available* to all. Appropriating that forgiveness comes by repentance. If your daughter has not accepted the forgiveness that gives her new birth into the family of God, now is the time to talk to her about it. If she is a Christian, a child of God, then she needs to go to God and ask to be restored to fellowship. Sin doesn't void our status as a child of God, but it does interfere with our relationship with him. Your daughter's pregnancy didn't void her status as your daughter, and the same is true spiritually. If she was a Christian before becoming pregnant, then she still is. Her actions that resulted in pregnancy do, however, interfere with her relationship with you, and those actions also interfere with her relationship with her spiritual father. The great news is that God is always waiting to receive and restore us. This was the point of the story of the prodigal son. God *wants* us to be in a right relationship with him, and he has made that possible through Jesus' death on the cross. Don't be afraid to invite your pastor or another Christian to help you and your daughter with spiritual restoration. One of the great privileges of being a Christian is to be able to comfort and encourage other persons.

Create a Non-threatening Environment

One of your priorities should be to cultivate an environment where your daughter can make rational, thoughtful decisions. This means establishing a non-threatening environment – a sort of neutral ground. Her relationship with her parents should be one of support and love, not one of antagonism. When we feel disappointed in our children it is easy to become critical and judgmental. I once heard a story that helped me to understand how to love even when we don't feel like loving. It was about a young boy that hit a man in the head with a snowball. The man discovered who the boy was and knew something about him. He appeared at the boy's home one day and left a package for him with his mother. When the lad returned home and opened the package he found a fishing rod. Imagine his astonishment when his mother told him who had delivered the package. His conscience troubled him until finally the young boy went to the man's office and took the fishing rod back. Surprised, the man asked the boy why he was returning the rod. The young boy replied, "Sir, I don't deserve it. You see, I'm the one that hit you in the head with the snowball." The man answered, "Son, I didn't give it to you because you deserved it; I gave it to you because you needed it." You may not feel like your daughter deserves a non-threatening environment, but she does need it. Here are some suggestions for cultivating a non-threatening environment:

- don't criticize her for being pregnant
- respect her privacy, allow her to ponder secret thoughts
- respect her feelings about the baby's father
- respect her views even if you disagree
- offer your help, but allow her to say no
- don't isolate her, include her in family activities
- don't pretend she's not pregnant.

As a part of creating a non-threatening environment you should let you daughter know that she has options. When Louise was back at college I assured her that we would come up and bring her home any time she wanted. This option to come home helped her relax and be less apprehensive. One night she called home at nine o'clock. She was crying and said, "I want to come home!" Nothing else would do. I was exhausted and had no desire to drive to the college, and I had an idea she might calm down given some time. I told her to start packing while I got dressed, and I added that I would call just before I left home to come pick her up. After we got off the telephone I sat in the living room hoping that I wouldn't actually need to go. After about fifteen minutes (still in my bathrobe) I called and told her I was getting ready to leave. She said, "Oh, it's okay; you don't need to come." She had settled down and actually sounded cheerful. The knowledge that I *would* come whenever she really needed me gave her comfort and helped her feel secure. Your daughter needs that same feeling of security, the knowledge that you will be there for her when she needs you.

Another option that should be discussed early is the option to decide, at a later date, whether to parent the baby or choose adoption. Since that decision doesn't need to be made right away, your daughter will be more relaxed knowing that she can make the decision in her own time and without pressure. It is important that the issue be introduced early so that she can use the available time to think carefully through her decision. It is equally important to emphasize to her that no decision needs to be made right away. Again, let her know that she has options available so that she doesn't worry needlessly about being stuck with only one choice.

Standing Behind Your Daughter – Don't Do It!

When we want to encourage another person in some endeavor we usually say, "I'm behind you." What we generally mean by that expression is that we encourage that person to proceed, and we'll be a cheerleader of sorts. A pregnant teenager doesn't need a cheerleader, she needs a paraclete (no, not parakeet!). Paraclete is a word that comes from two Greek words. The first is *kletos*, which means one who is called. The second is *para* which means alongside or in the vicinity of. Together they form paraclete, meaning literally "one called alongside." This word in the New Testament is translated as "comforter." This is the word Jesus used when he promised to send the Comforter (John 15:26). Your daughter needs people who will stand <u>beside</u> her, not behind her. People who stand beside are the ones who will get up under the load when it gets heavy. Paracletes are the ones who support others with actions, not words.

During my second semester in seminary I met a wonderful paraclete. His name is Ed Bolen, and at the time he was the grader for my New Testament class. My daughter's baby was about to be born right in the middle of final exams. We were all under great stress because of the situation in general, but also because we expected the baby to be born with physical and mental problems. I had gone to Ed to explain to him that I might not be able to get everything completed on time. As I was leaving I broke down and began crying – at high noon on the front steps of the seminary library! Ed realized that I was in no shape to take any exams, so he said simply, "You go home and take care of your family, I'll take care of your professors." Ed did something for me that I didn't have the composure or ability to do – he explained the situation to all my professors and arranged for me to take incompletes in all my courses. Ed got up under the load when it got too heavy for me. Your daughter will have times when she will need someone to get up under the load with her, too.

Keep Things on Course

Before you learned your daughter was pregnant there were other things going on in your lives. Her pregnancy need not bring a halt to everything else. It is true that her pregnancy will impact activities and change schedules, but it is not necessary that everything else be put on hold. If you have other children they have needs as well. One of your priorities should be to keep other family activities going as normally as possible. It will be therapeutic for all involved to "keep the show going." It will also be helpful for your daughter to know that her pregnancy has not totally disrupted everyone else's lives. There will come a time (labor and delivery) when all the family will be focused on the daughter who is carrying the baby, but until then your family should be able to carry on pretty well doing all the other things you would normally have do.

Regarding other children, you will undoubtedly be concerned about their reaction to having a sister who is pregnant and unmarried. You will probably discover that their response will be greatly influenced by your own. I can still remember when Louise broke the news to her sister, Sarah. Sarah came to me later that morning and didn't know whether she had heard correctly or was having a dream. We told Sarah that it was no dream (much as we might have wished it ourselves). We also assured Sarah that Louise was a part of our family and as such she would receive our support, prayers, and fellowship. It seemed that Sarah was "processing" this response. We as a family had never gone through a crisis like this before, and now Sarah would get a first hand look at what our response would be to a child in trouble. As it turned out, Sarah quickly became fully engaged in supporting and loving Louise. Perhaps children can better empathize with a sibling in trouble because they are closer in age than parents are to the children. Anyway, Sarah helped provide a supportive environment for Louise.

Your pregnant daughter needs to keep the show going, too. She has to do something during the pregnancy besides get big. Before Louise broke the news to us she was petrified that we would go through the ceiling. I would have expected us to as well, but we didn't. We felt shock, pain, and disappointment, but we had a sense that God would see us through it all. Then after Louise learned that we were supportive of her she was eager to return to college and finish the semester. She broke the news to us on a Friday night; the following Sunday evening I took her back to her dormitory. It seemed that staying in school during that semester would be the best thing for her to do. It gave her something to do, and it helped keep her life on track. It minimized the impact of this unexpected pregnancy, and it sure beat the other option – come home and sit around watching "talk shows." Louise was in a Christian college where she had lots of support and prayer partners. Those friends made it possible for her to finish her first semester of college in spite of the pregnancy.

Right now you might be struggling with the enormity of the situation. Don't allow the problems to overwhelm you. Remember that God is bigger than all our problems. As you seek God's guidance for the days ahead here are some questions that will help you. They are designed to help you think about the "big picture" instead of focusing on the present situation.

1. What were your daughter's plans before she discovered she was pregnant? It is not necessary to abandon these plans; instead you will discover that there will be ways to pursue them anyway.

2. What would you identify as your number one priority concerning your daughter and your family?

3. What other priorities would you identify?

4. What strengths does your family have that will help you in the days and weeks ahead?

5. Have you experienced situations in the past that looked hopeless but turned out okay?

6. What biblical stories illustrate God's power to turn a bad situation into good?

7. In what way might God use the present situation to bring blessings to your family?

As you discuss the questions above, think about how God has guided your lives in the past. Remind yourselves as parents (and your daughter) how God is mightier than all the problems we face. Finally, recall how God wants to work good for us, even when we stumble.

Chapter 3

Share the Burden

The body is a unit, though it is made up of many parts; and though all its parts are many, they form one body. So it is with Christ." 1 Corinthians 12:12

Teen pregnancy is a family event. By this I am not referring to cause or responsibility, but to effect. The parents and siblings of a pregnant teenager cannot simply pretend that nothing is happening. It affects every member of the family. Nor can the family members put their lives on hold for a year. All must continue with their own routines of work, school, and other activities. The thing is, whatever we do on a daily basis, we carry with us the emotional pain from problems at home. Because of this we can become preoccupied with personal problems to the point that our effectiveness at our daily tasks becomes impaired. So in order to keep our lives healthy and balanced, we need to enlist assistance when we face difficult problems.

Most of us do not like to admit to personal or family problems. We live in a society where personal accomplishment and control are highly esteemed. To admit to having a family problem is to confess loss of control. As a result we become reluctant to admit to having problems. We often decide to remain quite – keep the problem to ourselves and hope we can work things out. We keep our pain a personal secret. As things progress, the burden becomes greater and the cumulative effect of carrying the load alone takes its toll. Eventually we may either break down emotionally or withdraw in order to avoid admitting the problem to those around us. Neither of these options is healthy, and neither contributes to growing in our faith.

When we are under a load, it is healthy and proper to seek support and help from others. Parents can best help their daughter when they themselves are strengthened and healthy. When we receive encouragement and ministry from others, we are also reminded that others do care about and value us. Remember that God did not design us to bear our problems alone. In Galatians 6:2 Paul admonishes Christians to "Carry each other's burdens, and in this way you will fulfill the law of Christ." Even Jesus, when he was being led to His crucifixion, had help carrying the cross. We are all dependent upon one another in some way or other. Christians everywhere, like blood relatives, are family. While we may be reluctant to seek support, comfort, and help from other Christians, we need to remember that God has given Christians a duty to help one another. When we are in need, if we refuse to allow other Christians to help us, we deny them the opportunity to fulfill their calling to serve Christ by serving others.

Even when we resolve to admit our situation to those around us, we may fear that we will break down and cry when we actually do talk about it. One of the things I dreaded most was that in sharing my problem I would lose control of my emotions and start crying. Finally, I gave up resisting the urge to cry. What I discovered is that crying is actually very therapeutic. Real people do cry, and it's a great relief to stop pretending that we can always handle things without becoming emotional.

Just as your daughter needs affirmation and love, so do you as parents. At the time we discovered Louise's pregnancy, we were visiting several local churches. In typical Baptist fashion, we had filled out the guest card at a church one Sunday. That afternoon we received a call from a lady who was following up on our visit. She offered to come by to visit us and see if we had any questions about the church. Reluctantly, I decided to be up front about our situation. I told her we had just discovered our older daughter was pregnant, then I asked how she thought the people at that church would receive us. She began with, "Well, when it happened in our family. . . ." She then went on to tell us how the church had loved and cared for them when they experienced teen pregnancy. That what exactly what we needed to hear – and the person we needed to hear it from! I have since thought of that lady as our "angel," as I believe God specially chose her to minister to our need for affirmation at that time.

You should, of course, talk to your pastor. The pastor will normally have contacts with persons and agencies that will be helpful to you. Many churches today have established counseling ministries. Specially trained pastoral counselors can help you identify and deal with the emotional and spiritual issues you will face. Often they operate on a sliding-scale fee basis, charging according to one's ability to pay. If your church does not have a counseling ministry, ask your pastor or look in the telephone book under "Counselors." The purpose of counseling is not to dictate to you what you should do, but to help you discover the resources to make appropriate decisions yourselves.

One thing you should consider doing early is to get in contact with an agency that works with unmarried pregnant women. This might be an adoption agency, but a word of caution is in order here: it is important to allow your daughter to make the decision to choose adoption or not. Agencies which are under pressure to produce adoptable babies are not likely to be objective. When their "fee" depends on producing a baby for adoption, they will probably advise strongly in favor of that route. What your daughter will need (early) is unbiased information to help her arrive at a well-thought decision. Church-based agencies are not profit oriented, so they are more likely to be objective in providing information. Check with your own denomination (and others) about information for prospective birth mothers on both raising the child and on adoption.

Support for Yourselves

Once you understand why you need support and encouragement, where do you look? As already mentioned, begin at church – your pastor and Sunday School Class. Be aware that at times people may not know how to respond. While they may want to be supportive, they are unsure of what to say or whether to even discuss the subject. It will be helpful for them if you will tell them that it's okay to talk about the situation. Give them permission to bring up the subject and ask how you and your children are doing. Once people know that you are willing to talk about things, they will be more comfortable approaching you. They won't feel that they are invading your private space.

Another place to seek help is your church's youth leader if there is a separate person for that job. A knowledgeable youth leader will probably be more in tune with what teenagers are facing today than most parents.

The youth leader is also likely to have a special understanding of your child's feelings and concerns. This person will likely be able to help you better understand and communicate with your daughter. Your daughter's Sunday School teacher can also be a good source of information about youth in general and your own daughter.

Finally, don't forget parents who have gone through the experience of bringing a child through an unwed pregnancy. I have often heard that the most valuable counselors for alcoholics are former alcoholics. The principle is that those who have walked in your shoes already know the pitfalls, the pain, and ways to work through the problem. Parents who have been where you find yourself likely to have a special place in their hearts for you. They not only are able to help and encourage you, but they usually will be glad to do so. You may know such persons personally. If not, ask around. Crisis pregnancy centers may be able to refer you to parents who have "been there." They may even have a parent support group. If not, they might well be willing to start one.

Telling Family

Other family members will, of course, eventually discover your daughter's pregnancy. At one time it was not unusual to keep such news hidden from family. Keeping these kinds of secrets though is difficult; things like that often surface whether we want them to or not. Besides, keeping secrets from family puts additional emotional stress on you. Perpetuating the secret requires care in what is said at family gatherings and worry about whether someone else who knows will "slip up." The decision to keep the secret also assumes that other family members (the ones who don't know) will be unable to cope with the news, unwilling to accept it, or in some other way not up to the task of dealing with the truth. We forget, though, that every other person we know has had his or her own share of dealing with problems. No one escapes the realities of living in a world affected by sin. Sometimes we want to shield our own parents from the pain of knowing their granddaughter is pregnant when she's not supposed to be. That was the case in our family – we were reluctant to disappoint them. Even so, we told them early that Louise was pregnant. The reality for us was that the older folk were far less traumatized that my wife and I were. They had been around longer, experienced more of the reality of life, and learned long ago that things like this happen. As it turned out, they were supportive and accepting instead of shocked and dismayed. I still remember what my father-in-law said when I told him by telephone: "Well, tell Louise we love her." And he meant it.

While you don't want to advertise in the newspaper, your close family members should be told about your daughter's pregnancy. Besides relieving you of the burden of carrying the secret, it gives them the opportunity to express their love and care. They may also offer advice. If they do, accept their offer as evidence of their genuine concern. You may not choose to act on everything they suggest, and you should not feel that you are obligated to do so. They may even disagree (strongly) on some of the decisions that have to eventually be made, like the choice of adoption or raising the child. My advice here: respect their feelings, but do not obligate yourself to their suggestions. You and your daughter will be the ones who will be most affected by the decisions that are made, so she and you are the ones who should be the ultimate decision makers.

Be Encouraged

Elizabeth Elliot is a well-known Christian personality with a nationally syndicated radio program. As a young bride she followed her husband to South America where he was following God's leading to mission work. Soon after arriving, Jim Elliot and his companions were killed by the Indian tribe they had gone to evangelize. Elizabeth knows suffering, too. Yet she always opens her radio program with the same words: "You are loved with an everlasting love." Every time I hear her speak these words I am strengthened and encouraged. It's not simply a catchy phrase that is so meaningful to me, but the reality behind it. Those words are a reminder that God loved me from the beginning of creation, and he has never stopped and never will. God loves you, too. I know all too well how easy it is to question God's love during difficult times. When we were going through Louise's pregnancy, I questioned whether God even knew I was alive, much less hurting. Fortunately, God is big enough to handle our questions and doubts. We have since been able to look back on our experience and see that God never left our side. Even when we didn't feel it, he was there. And right now God loves you, too – with an everlasting love. He is by your side, and for that you can be encouraged.

You may ask, "If God loves me so much, why does he allow this pain in my life?" I won't pretend to give you a simple answer, because

I don't have one. But there is something I can relate that helps put the question in perspective. When our children were young we took them to the doctor for the normal series of shots. When our younger daughter, Sarah, was about ready to begin school, we took her in for her first such experience. Anne, my wife, got Sarah all excited by telling her she was going to get her immunizations. Sarah loved it; she was special and was about to get special treatment. She even bragged that she was going to get her "immunizations." Louise, the older and wiser at age eight or so, knew better. She warned Sarah that she was going to get "shots," and that they would hurt. Sarah was unimpressed. She was going to get her *immunizations*, and she was proud of it. She walked briskly into the doctor's office with a big smile on her face. Even when the nurse approached her arm with the needle she was smiling. But when that needle went into her arm Sarah's expression changed instantly. Her face seemed to say, "That was no immunization – that was a *shot!* " Sarah might not have understood why her parents allowed that pain to come into her life either, but you and I as parents know that sometimes pain is necessary to pave the way for healthy growth.

We may not understand why God allows pain to come into our lives. Even so, God loves us. We know he loves us because of the Cross. Because Jesus died for our sin, we can be assured that whatever happens, God loves us. And because Jesus was resurrected from death, we know that God keeps his promises. A favorite hymn of mine goes, "Because He lives, I can face tomorrow." So be encouraged. Even if you don't quite know how things will turn out, you can know that God loves you and God is in ultimate control. Because He lives, you can face tomorrow, too.

Cast all your anxiety on him because he cares for you (1 Pet. 5:7).

Epilog

We all want to know the ending of the story, and when we are going through a crisis we want to know how things are going to turn out. We are anxious for answers, but often times we have to learn to wait for answers. I have been surprised at how frequently persons ask us how things turned out for our daughter, so I will take a few moments to share with you about that.

Louise took the second semester of her college career off because that was when she delivered the baby. She did work in a day-care center though up until near time to go to the hospital. Choosing adoption was a healthy decision, but it was painful. Getting to know the adoptive parents a little bit helped greatly. It gave her inner assurance that the decision she made was in fact good for the child, that she would have a loving and caring home. Louise had a private dedication service for the baby which helped bring closure to her experience. This was conducted in a local church and included the adoptive parents and a few friends. It was a time for all of us to acknowledge the life that God had created and how very much we all loved that child. The adoptive parents participated, and the entire experience was a very significant event for us all.

There was another period of about six months after delivery until the healing process had brought us all to a point of feeling healthy again. Since then Louise has worked as a volunteer in a crisis pregnancy center here in Louisville whenever she was home from college. Her first semester back at college was not as easy as we had wished, but Louise worked hard. In the end, she finished college making the dean's list for her last two years. Through her experience Louise has grown in maturity and in her faith. Recently she was married to a fine Christian man whom she met in college, and they are beginning their lives as young adults together.

You will be eager for your daughter to move on with her life as well, as were we. We have learned that time is a part of the process of healing and growing. Give yourselves time to heal after the baby is born. When we expect instant results, we become disappointed. Instead, trust God to bring healing and growth in his time. This will be a time of growing in faith for you. I don't like to wait, and maybe you don't either. I become impatient with God when his schedule is not the same as mine. Over the years though I have learned that God's foreknowledge is greater than mine could ever be. When I was in the Marine Corps I was a helicopter pilot. Once we were flying to New Orleans from northern Florida. We were flying in clouds and could not see fifty feet in any direction, so we were completely dependent on the radar controllers on the ground. At one point in the trip they had us turn off of the airway (an electronic highway in the sky), and they guided us in a semi-circle until we got back on the airway. This was inconvenient and time-consuming; we were in a hurry to get to New Orleans because we had already had a long and tiring day. Anyway, the reason they guided us around the "long way" was that there was a thunder cloud on the airway just ahead of us. They could see it on their radar, but we couldn't see it. Because of their greater ability to see what was ahead, they were able to safely get us around a dangerous obstacle. God also has greater vision than we have. He will sometimes take us the long way because it is the safe way or the way to grow. In any case, God's way is not for lack of love, but because of his infinite love and foreknowledge. When you sometimes question God's presence with you (as you probably will), remember that he is always there and will always take you the best way. It may only be later that you are able to see the evidence of his loving hand.

National Organizations

The following service organizations provide either direct pregnancy counseling or services to pregnancy centers throughout the United States. You may locate a local pregnancy counseling center in your area by call one of the organizations below.

- **American Life League**
  PO Box 1350
  Stafford, VA 22555
  540-659-4171

- **Bethany Christian Services**
  PO Box 294
  Grand Rapids, MI 49501
  800-224-7610
  616-459-6273

- **CARENET**
  109 Carpenter Dr., Ste. 100
  Sterling, VA 20164
  703-478-5661

- **Heartbeat International**
  7870 Olentangy River Road, Ste. 304
  Columbus, OH 43235
  614-885-7577

- **National Life Center**
  686 North Broad St.
  Woodbury, NJ 08096
  800-848-5683
  609-848-1819

- **The Nurturing Network**
  200 Clocktower Place
  Suite 200-A PO Box 223099
  Carmel, CA 93922
  800-848-1819

Unsung Heros

Every day they report to their duty stations. We rarely hear about them or what they do, yet their work is vitally important to persons who are hurting, confused, and feel alone with a problem. They talk to people every day whom they've never met and may never meet. Still, they do the best they can to be a friend during a time of need. They take classes on their own time to learn how to do their work, and most of them are not paid – they are volunteers. Day in and day out they are on duty so that someone in need will have a friend to speak with. I am talking about the tens of thousands of volunteer and staff workers in crisis pregnancy centers all over the country.

Our daughter visited a crisis pregnancy center afraid that her fears might be true. They were. But at the center she found a friend, someone who would love her and comfort her. Last year I called the center where my daughter had gone and spoke with the director. I thanked her that the center and workers were there when my daughter needed them. The director didn't remember my daughter though. I'm not surprised. They see many, many young women, often on a moment's notice. Recently I was visiting a local center for a visit with the director who is a friend of mine. At first we had some time to chat, but soon the phone started ringing. First one call, then another. An appointment, a follow-up call, a girl who needed comforting. This particular center doesn't just talk to girls. They keep a store room of supplies to hand out when needed – baby clothes, car seats, diapers, whatever might be needed. They also keep a supply of literature to hand-out to girls and their parents. All for free. No charge, nothing asked. They don't ask because they are there to serve.

Most crisis pregnancy centers operate on shoe-string budgets. They have mostly volunteer workers. Partly because it is a labor of love, but also because they don't have money for salaries. We have a new thirty-million dollar (more I think) football stadium being built right now. There seems to be no trouble getting money for a football stadium, but places where real ministry takes place day in and day out, those places hold a bake sale or whatever else they can do to raise money to keep the telephone line connected and the doors open. They may have a list of donors, but they still have to watch expenditures closely. They do whatever they can to be there when needed.

It may be that a crisis pregnancy center was there for your daughter and, indirectly, for your family. Young women may only visit a center one or two times, but those one or two visits are crucial at the time they are needed. I have often wondered where our daughter could have turned if no center had been available. She was out of town at college. We, her parents, were not there, but in looking back, I am convinced that the center was the best place for her to learn the news. Center workers are trained to be both understanding and helping. I'm not sure I could have been either at first.

If your daughter has been helped by the caring CPC workers, ordinary people doing an extraordinary job, it may be that at some time you might want to make a contribution to that work. There are several ways you can help out. Here are some suggestions.

1. A word of thanks: crisis pregnancy center workers encounter crises daily; they would certainly appreciate knowing how their contribution has helped someone.

2. You may, as our own daughter did, wish to offer to help as a volunteer worker. There always seems to be a shortage of help. You don't have to make a large commitment either; they will accept whatever time you have to offer.

3. If you are able, a financial contribution would always be helpful. As I said, they do not ask anything at all of the girls they help. Yet they are there to give whatever support they can – literature, books, food, clothing, etc.

God has given us loving and compassionate people who devote their time, energy, and resources to provide a ministry for young women in need. Let us thank God and those workers for the wonderful job they do each and every day.

Your Comments Are Appreciated

Your feedback is important. We continually strive to improve our ministry literature, so we encourage you to let us know what you think of this book and other Good Life Publishing material. Use this form and mail to us at the address at the bottom. Thank you for taking the time to write us.

Good Life Publishing
PO Box 6925
Louisville, KY 40206
E-mail: feedback@GLPub.com

To order additional copies of this book, use the form below and mail with payment to:

Good Life Publishing
PO Box 6925
Louisville, KY 40206
502-491-6565

ITEM	Quantity	Price Ea	Total
Help for Hurting Parents		$3.95	
Whose Child is This? — *A Biblical View of Adoption*		$0.95	
		sub-total	
Kentucky residents: sales tax	6% of	sub-total	
Shipping			$3.50
sub-total + sales tax + shipping	ORDER	TOTAL	

Ship to:

Name: _____

Address: _____

City, State Zip_____

You can also reach us by E-mail at: books@GLPub.com.

Be sure to visit our Internet site at

WWW.GLPub.COM